J.R.R. Tolkien

by Alexandra Wallner

illustrated by John Wallner

A boy on a magic pen Lion START brings him in

Holiday House / New York

The publisher wishes to thank Dr. Jeffrey Bourns
of Harvard University for reviewing the text and art for accuracy.

HOLIDAY HOUSE is registered in the U.S. Patent and Trademark Office.
Printed and Bound in April 2011 at Tien Wah Press, Johor Bahru, Johor, Malaysia.
The text typeface is Hightower.
The illustrations were created with watercolor, colored pencil, and ink on Lana watercolor paper.
www.holidayhouse.com
First Edition
1 3 5 7 9 10 8 6 4 2

Library of Congress Cataloging-in-Publication Data
Wallner, Alexandra.
J.R.R. Tolkien / by Alexandra Wallner ; illustrated by John Wallner. — 1st ed.
p. cm.
ISBN 978-0-8234-1951-7 (hardcover)
1. Tolkien, J. R. R. (John Ronald Reuel), 1892-1973—Pictorial works—Juvenile literature.
2. Authors, English—20th century—Biography—Juvenile literature. I. Wallner, John C. II. Title.
PR6039.O32Z892 2011
828'.91209—dc22
[B]
2009006044

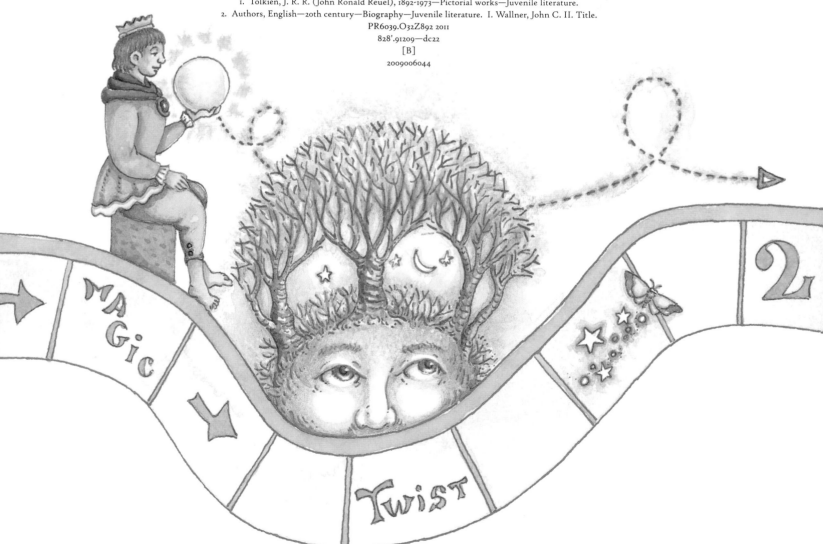

To all storytellers who fire our imaginations
—A. W.

To the Game
of
Imagination
J.C.W.

and

all

the

Twists

and

Turns

Lose
1
Turn

Africa
Move
Forward

John Ronald Reuel Tolkien was born to English parents in a hot, dusty town in South Africa, where his father worked.

Their house was by the *veldt*, or open field. Ronald's parents warned him that wolves, wild dogs, jackals, and lions prowled there. They also told him about snakes and spiders in the woodshed; but even so, one time a hairy black tarantula bit him. Another time the neighbor's monkeys climbed over the garden wall and chewed up three of his shirts.

When Ronald was three, his mother took him and his baby brother, Hilary, for a visit to England. While they were there, they got the terrible news that the boys' father had died.

Countryside

Birmingham

Go Back
2 Spaces

Play

Their mother did not take Ronald and Hilary back to Africa. Instead they moved to the green, leafy countryside near the city of Birmingham.

Their house was pleasant. It had a tangle of plants in the garden and stood on a quiet lane. Nearby were ponds, woods, and fields of wild flowers for Ronald and Hilary to play in. There were also narrow paths with names such as Hob Lane.

Adventure
Move
2 spaces

Hob
Lane

The family was poor, but Ronald's mother knew many things. So, instead of sending her sons to school, which would cost money, she taught them at home. Ronald played with making up words and drew lots of dragons.

When Ronald and Hilary were older, their mother enrolled them in a school in Birmingham, so they moved to the city. In their house, Ronald sat by the window of his room upstairs and looked out over the sooty rooftops. The dirty, noisy city was so different from the green, quiet countryside. But there was a patch of grass near the railway tracks. He often went there to sit and would say out loud the strange names on the boxcars from the country of Wales. He enjoyed the unusual sounds of the words, so different from English.

Nantyglo

Senghenydd

Blaen-Rhondda

Strange
Names

Secret
PLACE

Next

At school, Ronald soon made friends with the other boys. He studied the science of words, called philology, and even invented his own language. He shared it with his friends, and they wrote secret notes to each other that no one else could understand. He was also finding time to write stories.

His mother had been sick for some time and died when Ronald was a teenager. Ronald and Hilary were devastated.

Their new guardian was a priest whom their mother had known. He sent them to live with their aunt.

But Ronald and Hilary didn't like living with their aunt. They told their guardian, and he arranged for them to live in a boardinghouse. There, Ronald met a pretty young woman named Edith Bratt, who was also an orphan. They often talked for hours. But Ronald was only eighteen and Edith was twenty-one. When his guardian learned of their friendship, he found another place for Ronald and Hilary to live. He wanted Ronald to study, not think about Edith. He told Ronald not to see her or write to her until he was twenty-one. Ronald did as he was told but wrote in his diary, "Three years is awful."

Ronald studied hard and was accepted into Oxford University. He would now be able to study old languages and to write. He made new friends there who also wrote. They formed a club to read one another's stories. Ronald often made up stories about elves.

Once on a trip to Switzerland, he bought a postcard showing an old man talking to a white fawn. He kept it folded in a piece of paper on which he wrote, "Origin of Gandalf." One day he would write about this character with magical powers.

Ronald also invented more languages. He wrote poems and stories and illustrated them. A friend asked him what they were about. Ronald answered, "I don't know. I'll try to find out."

New Letters

A B C

OLD
LETTERS
MO

í ć m
í m ħ ť à
í ť à

19

Soon, though, World War I began. Ronald left school and enlisted in the army, where he learned about Morse code, flag signaling, and signal rockets. He enjoyed using these codes because they were different ways to send messages—almost like using new languages.

Ronald never forgot Edith. On the very night that he turned twenty-one, he wrote to her and asked her to marry him. They were married before Ronald was sent to France to fight.

Fighting in the trenches was terrible. Working in the rain and mud, Ronald got a fever and spent many months in a hospital in England. Sadly, some of his friends from the writing club at Oxford who were also soldiers died in the war. They would never write any more stories. One of them had once written to Ronald, "May you say the things I have tried to say long after I am not there to say them." It was now up to Ronald to write the best stories he could.

Many changes

Some Good Some BAD

Bag's End

But at the same time he had a wife to support, as well as a baby son, their first child. So when he left the army, he got a job working on a dictionary. One day, he caught a bad cold. To recover, he went to an aunt's farm, called Bag's End. He wrote the name in his notebook. Perhaps he could use it in a story.

Ronald thought that there were not enough legends about England, so he started writing his own. He kept notes in a book that he titled *The Book of Lost Tales*. He wrote a story about a time when there were elves who were artists and writers. He invented a language for them to speak. When he did not know the meaning of a word he had made up, he wrote, "What does this mean? I must find out."

ELVES

Words

Write a Story and Move 2 Spaces.

Stories

A few years later, Ronald became a professor at Oxford University. He and his wife now had four children: John, Michael, Christopher, and Priscilla. Ronald loved to tell them stories. Each Christmas he wrote them letters telling news from Father Christmas and his helpers at the North Pole.

But still he felt he didn't have enough time to write the stories he wanted to. One night, tired and bored, when he was grading a student's notebook, he turned a page and found a blank space. On it he wrote, "In a hole in the ground there lived a hobbit." Later he said, "I thought I'd better find out what hobbits were like."

A Hole in the Ground

Hobbit ?

Goblin

D

A → ᚣ

B → Φ

C → ᚠ

MORE

He wrote about Bilbo Baggins, a creature who is not quite human and has pointed ears and furry feet. Bilbo lives in a house that's built into the side of a hill. The house is called Bag's End, just like Ronald's aunt's house. Bilbo knows a wizard named Gandalf, who sends Bilbo on many adventures.

Bilbo is ordinary but has courage against impossible odds. In that way the hobbit might have been Ronald. He too was ordinary but had great courage during his childhood and while fighting in the war.

And so *The Hobbit* was written and published as a children's book. But adults loved it, too.

Young readers wanted more stories about the hobbit, but Ronald didn't have any. He was writing a long story called *The Lord of the Rings*, a made-up legend that has hobbits in it but is not a children's story. The story is about the adventures of Frodo and Sam, hobbits who face many dangers. Gandalf appears in it again. Some of the characters speak in languages such as Elvish, which Ronald had invented.

Ronald rewrote the story many times to make it perfect. Even his son Christopher helped him rewrite it. Finally, sixteen years later, it was finished.

1948

1950

1954

LORD of the RINGS

A ← Little More

It was a long story that took three books to tell. Many people loved it, and it was printed in other languages. Some people loved Ronald's story so much, they formed a club called the Tolkien Society. Ronald became so famous that he was invited to meet the queen of England.

Ronald led an ordinary life. He once wrote, "I am in fact a hobbit in all but size. I like gardens, trees, and . . . farmlands. I smoke a pipe, and like good plain food. . . . I am fond of mushrooms. . . . I go to bed late and get up late. . . . I do not travel much." But when we read Ronald's books, we step inside his imagination—which was anything but ordinary.

Bilbo Baggins

Twist

END

START
AGAIN

TIME LINE

1892	John Ronald Reuel Tolkien is born in Bloemfontein, South Africa, January 3.
1894	Ronald's brother, Hilary, is born.
1896	Ronald and Hilary's father dies. Family moves to the countryside in Sarehole, Warwickshire, England.
1900	The family moves to a suburb of Birmingham, where Ronald attends school.
1904	Ronald and Hilary's mother dies.
1908	Ronald meets Edith Bratt in the boardinghouse where he and Hilary live.
1911	Ronald becomes a student at Oxford University.
1914	World War I begins.
1915	Ronald graduates from Oxford.
1916	Ronald and Edith are married, March 22. Ronald, in the army, is sent to France. Ronald develops a fever and is sent home.
1917	Son John is born.
1918	World War I ends. Ronald gets a job as a lexicographer (a person who helps write a dictionary).
1920	Ronald gets a job at Leeds University. Son Michael is born.
1924	Son Christopher is born.
1925	Ronald becomes a professor at Oxford.
1929	Daughter Priscilla is born.
1937	*The Hobbit* is published.
1954	*The Lord of the Rings*, first two books, are published.
1955	*The Lord of the Rings*, third book, is published.
1971	Edith dies.
1973	Ronald dies.
1976	*The Father Christmas Letters* is published.

BIBLIOGRAPHY

Carpenter, Humphrey. *J. R. R. Tolkien: A Biography*. Rev. ed. New York: Houghton Mifflin, 2000.

——, ed., with the assistance of Christopher Tolkien. *The Letters of J. R. R. Tolkien*. New York: Houghton Mifflin, 2000.

Shippey, T. A. *J. R. R. Tolkien: Author of the Century*. New York: Houghton Mifflin, 2002.

SOURCE NOTES

All quotations come from *J. R. R. Tolkien: A Biography* by Humphrey Carpenter.

p. 16	"Three years is awful." p. 51
p. 18	"Origin of Gandalf" p. 59
	"I don't know. I'll try to find out." p. 83
p. 21	"May you say the things I have tried to say . . ." p. 94
p. 22	"What does this mean? I must find out." p. 102
p. 24	"In a hole in the ground there lived a hobbit." p. 175
	"I thought I'd better find out what hobbits were like." p. 175
p. 30	"I am in fact a hobbit in all but size. . . ." p. 179